PLANT
FACTS

by
William Anthony

BEARPORT
PUBLISHING

Minneapolis, Minnesota

Library of Congress Cataloging-in-Publication Data

Names: Anthony, William, 1996- author.
Title: Plant facts / William Anthony.
Description: Fusion books. | Minneapolis, Minnesota : Bearport Publishing
Company, [2022] | Series: Fact-o-graphics! | Includes bibliographical
references and index.
Identifiers: LCCN 2021005278 (print) | LCCN 2021005279 (ebook) | ISBN
9781647479893 (library binding) | ISBN 9781647479947 (paperback) | ISBN
9781647479992 (ebook)
Subjects: LCSH: Plants—Juvenile literature.
Classification: LCC QK49 .A58 2022 (print) | LCC QK49 (ebook) | DDC
581.3—dc23
LC record available at https://lccn.loc.gov/2021005278
LC ebook record available at https://lccn.loc.gov/2021005279

For more information, write to Bearport Publishing, 5357 Penn
Avenue South, Minneapolis, MN 55419. Printed in the United
States of America.

Photo credits:
4 - Man As Thep, 5 - Ian 2010, Anna Frajtova, rolandtopor, 6 - herain
kanthatham, Vector Tradition, Amanita Silvicora, Thomas Pajot,
7 - kamomeen, Nik Merkulov, Tartila, Javid Kheyrabadi, 8 - Arnold O. A.
Pinto, 9 - Serp, Artens, 10 - Triff, 11 -bmphotographer,
Victor Metelskiy Iabzazuza, VactorPlotnikoff,
12 - Amanita Silvicora, Kingsly, 13 - Tshooter, oversnap,
14 - Tree of Life, Krzysztof Odziomek, curiosity,
Natali Snailcat, Nadzin, 15 - richcarey, 16 - Christian
Vinces, Ivana Milic, Beskova Ekaterina, 17 - gionnixxx,
BlueRingMedia, Pogorelova Olga, 18 - szefei,
davemhuntphotography, Kirasolly, aliaksei kruhlenia,
19 - jipatafoto89, 20 - Wealthylady, Gavran333,
Valentina Razumova, AN NGUYEN, light_s, 21 - Ariel
Bravy, 22 - Naeblys, Jannick Tessier, Alena Haurylik,
MSSA, practicuum, 23 - Cathy Keifer, Natali Snailcat.

Images are courtesy of Shutterstock.com. With
thanks to Getty Images, Thinkstock Photo and
iStockphoto.

CONTENTS

PLANT LIFE

Plants are living things, just like us. They can live on land or in water.

Plants make their own food using air, water, sunlight, and **nutrients** from the soil.

Plants can be food for animals and people. They also help us by putting **oxygen** in the air we breathe.

The main parts of a plant are the roots, stem, and leaves.

Trees are plants that have large stems called trunks. They have branches, too.

Branch

Leaves get energy from the sun to make food.

Trunk

The stem holds the plant up. It sends water and nutrients to the leaves.

Roots hold the plant in the ground. They take in water and nutrients.

5

FLOWERS

Many plants have flowers. Flowers are usually colorful, which draws in bugs. Then, the bugs **pollinate** the flowers. This helps the plants make seeds, fruits, and new plants.

Did you know that broccoli is a flower?

Scientists think plants started growing flowers around 130 million years ago. That's in the time of the dinosaurs!

Some flowers grow on other plants. They don't need soil. They get what they need to live from the air around them.

The corpse lily can grow more than 3 feet (1 m) wide. It got its name because it smells like rotting meat!

TREES

Trees are tall plants with leaves. Many trees have leaves that change with the seasons. Their leaves fall off in winter and grow back in spring.

Spring

Summer

Fall

Plants like this that are not tall enough to be trees are called shrubs.

Evergreen trees keep their leaves all year.

Winter

All year

In the fall, trees make less food and their leaves lose their green color.

The average tree has enough wood to make around 170,000 pencils.

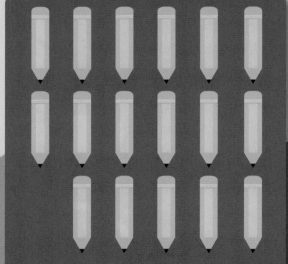

= 10,000 pencils

You can tell the age of a tree from the rings in its trunk. Each ring is a year in the tree's life.

A baobab tree can have enough water in its trunk to fill more than 650 baths!

The heaviest thing on Earth is a tree! The giant sequoia tree can weigh more than 6,000 tons (5,400 metric tons).

GRASSES

Grasses are plants that cover yards, parks, and fields.

Different grasses grow in different places. There is grass on mountains, in deserts, and even under the sea!

Elephant grass grows in Africa. It got its name because it grows tall enough to hide an elephant.

Grasses can be used to build things.

Grasses are food for many animals. Cows, deer, panda bears, and more eat grass!

Did you know that bamboo is a grass?

UNDERWATER PLANTS

Plants also grow underwater. Plants need sunlight, so most plants live closer to the surface of the water where there is plenty of sun.

Some plants in lakes or rivers live just partly in the water.

Plants that live in water can be **shelter** and food for fish.

There are many different underwater plants. Some are big, and some are tiny.

Seagrass is the only plant with flowers that can grow in the ocean.

Kelp plants can grow more than 200 ft (61 m) tall. That's as tall as 20 school buses stacked on top of one another!

The smallest ocean plants are too tiny to see with the human eye.

CACTI

Cacti are plants that live in hot deserts with little rain. But they still need water to live. So, they save water in their roots, stems, and leaves.

A cactus's leaves are actually needles. They protect the plant from animals.

Cacti can live for more than a year without rain!

Some cacti can be eaten. But take off the needles first!

Cacti can live to be up to 200 years old!

There are close to 2,000 **species** of cacti.

17

RAIN FORESTS

Rain forests are very warm and rainy. They are home to more than half of all the kinds of plants and animals that live on Earth.

Some rain forests get more than an inch (2.5 cm) of rain every day!

The plants of the rain forest give shelter to many animals, including frogs.

The Amazon in South America is the largest rain forest in the world. It is about the size of the United States, minus Alaska and Hawaii.

There are about 16,000 different tree species in the Amazon.

Rain forest trees grow close together. When taller trees die and fall down, smaller trees grow to fill the empty space.

Bananas, chocolate, and pineapples come from rain forests like the Amazon.

Pineapple

FRUITS AND VEGGIES

Fruits and veggies are the parts of plants that we eat. Most veggies come from the roots, stem, or leaves of a plant. Fruits come from the flowers of a plant. They have seeds.

Heads of lettuce are leaves, celery is a stem, carrots are roots, and artichokes are flowers.

Unlike most fruits, strawberries have seeds on the outside. Each berry has around 200 seeds.

Apples have a lot of air in them. This is why apples can float in water.

EXTREME PLANTS

Some plants are **extreme**! They may be very big.
They may look strange or live in surprising places.

A tree found in an African rain forest is so big that it weighs about the same as 15 African elephants.

The dragon's blood tree gets its name from its red sap. The sap looks like blood!

Welwitschia is a desert plant that can live for up to 1,500 years.

Some plants can live in soil made superhot by volcanoes!

Before the 1500s, carrots were purple or yellow—not orange.

Many animals eat plants. But some plants eat animals!

GLOSSARY

extreme far beyond what is usual or expected

nutrients things that plants, animals, and people need to live and grow

oxygen something in the air that is needed for life

pollinate to pass on part of a plant to another plant of the same kind, so the plants can grow

shelter a place that provides safety from danger

species a group of very similar animals or plants that can create young together

INDEX